DURHAM RAILWAYS AROUND THE END OF THE 20TH CENTURY

RICHARD ALLEN

AMBERLEY

This book is dedicated to my close friend Joseph Boal, whose knowledge and enthusiasm for the railways and general history of the county encouraged me to visit many of these locations.

First published 2021

Amberley Publishing
The Hill, Stroud,
Gloucestershire, GL5 4EP

www.amberley-books.com

ISBN: 978 1 3981 0374 0 (print)
ISBN: 978 1 3981 0375 7 (ebook)

British Library Cataloguing in Publication Data.
A catalogue record for this book is available from the British Library.

Typeset in 10pt on 13pt Celeste.
Origination by Amberley Publishing.
Printed in the UK.

Contents

Introduction

I lived in north-east England between 1988 and 2003, which was a time when the area and its railways went through a number of significant changes, in particular ECML electrification and the closure of all the deep coal mines in the area.

Railway photography has always been my principal free-time occupation and I spent as much time as possible out on the railway with my camera. As with so many people, my interest was simply recording the passing scene but it quickly became obvious that the railway scene would soon change for ever and in some cases it became a race against time to record the old before it was replaced by the new. This particularly applied to the Leamside line, which had been retained as a diversionary route during ECML electrification and had little traffic otherwise. It had been strongly rumoured, and it was later confirmed, that the line would be closed on completion of the ECML electrification.

Despite the Beeching closures, the railway scene in County Durham remained full of interest in the late 1980s and throughout the 1990s. Freight, in particular coal, traffic was still buoyant until the last mines closed in the early 1990s. In addition, the Sectorisation policy of British Rail led to a multitude of new liveries, rather than the rather drab Rail Blue, which tended to fade over time and often looked very scruffy. Many lines retained semaphore signalling, adding to the interest.

One particular feature of the railway scene in the area during 1988 and 1989 was the appearance of loco-hauled 'Pacer replacer' trains using rakes of three or four coaches, as the new class 143s were proving to be very unreliable. The majority of these workings used class 47/4s or 31/4s but various other locos would occasionally turn up. These ceased at the end of the summer 1989 timetable.

I have taken the scope of this book to cover the old county of Durham between the Tees and the Tyne, including those parts that were transferred to Cleveland and Tyne and Wear in 1974. I have tried to include some of the lesser-known areas and workings wherever possible – hence the paucity of class 91s in the ECML chapter! I have also covered the lesser-known lines and areas at the expense of the ECML, which has been well covered elsewhere.

I have included brief descriptions of the lines in question but they are not intended to be comprehensive and there are many books available for those who wish to learn a bit more about the railways of the fascinating area. I have also not described the history and operations of the Weardale Railway except in passing.

All opinions expressed in this book are my own and equally, any errors are my own.

1

The East Coast Main Line

The principal railway in the county was and remains the East Coast Main Line. Today's route dates from 1872 when the line from Tursdale Junction through Durham to Gateshead was opened. Over the years, the majority of local stations have closed, leaving only three open in the county: Darlington, Durham and Chester-le-Street.

The line crosses the River Tees from Yorkshire into County Durham on a viaduct just south of the site of Croft Spa station. Lineside signs advise the traveller that they have passed from Yorkshire into County Durham.

The site of Croft Spa station (closed 3 March 1969) is just north of the viaduct. Following the withdrawal of local services north of York on 15 September 1958, it had been served only by trains between Darlington and Richmond. The station has disappeared without trace.

A few minutes later, northbound trains arrive at the spectacular Darlington station, once known as Darlington Bank Top. The line from Middlesbrough trails in from the east and a disused turntable can be seen on the west side just south of the station. There was also a very 1930s LNER signal box; the lower storey remains as a relay room. At one time, it was common to see locomotives stabled in the sidings at the south end but this is now very rare.

The station is located on a loop west of the main line. Very few expresses do not stop at Darlington these days and the avoiding lines are largely used by freight trains.

Darlington station is by far the most spectacular in the county and is rightly listed Grade II*. It opened on 1 July 1887 as the final part of a major upgrade to the railway facilities in the area.

Leaving Darlington, trains head north over the site of 'S & D Crossing', where the Stockton & Darlington line crossed the ECML on the level and very shortly after that the line is in open country. Aycliffe station closed on 2 March 1953 and no trace remains apart from the name 'Station Terrace' on a terrace of former railway houses, which are briefly glimpsed on the Down side of the line from a passing train. Just north of Aycliffe, the line passed under the once electrified Shildon–Newport line, which is also mentioned in chapters 3 and 7. The next station, Bradbury, closed on 2 January 1950 and its site is marked by an open space on the Down side immediately south of the bridge taking the railway over the A689 road from the A1(M) motorway (which can be seen to the west) to Hartlepool. The site is used as an access point for Network Rail staff and contractors.

Shortly after Bradbury, the line from Stockton can be seen approaching from the east and an LNER cut-out sign can be seen with the single word 'Stockton'. This joins the ECML at Ferryhill South Junction, where the line becomes quadruple track through the site of Ferryhill (closed 6 March 1967). The only clue as to the station's existence is the former goods shed on the Down side of the line. The station consisted of an island platform reached from the bridge that crosses the railway at this point. Ferryhill station was sufficiently far away from the settlement of the same name that a new community grew up around the station called 'Ferryhill Station'. This practice of naming a community after a station was not uncommon in the North East. The signal box here was of 1960s brick construction and after the electrification and associated resignalling of the ECML, only controlled the line to Stockton until it was decommissioned on 31 January 2021 as part of the Durham Coast resignalling scheme.

Ferryhill was once a major junction station with branches to Bishop Auckland, Hartlepool, Coxhoe Goods and Chilton Colliery, plus a short stub to Thrislington Colliery. The last of these to survive was a section of the Hartlepool line as far as Raisby Hill quarry, which closed in the early 1990s and is also described in chapter 8.

North of Ferryhill, the line enters a deep cutting with the Thrislington magnesite quarry on the up side. Around 2 miles north of Ferryhill, the quadruple track ends at Tursdale Junction and the course of the Leamside line can be seen heading north. As this was the first line to be built, it follows a straight line and the present ECML curves to the west as it heads for Durham.

Croxdale station (closed 26 September 1938) was in a cutting north of the old Great North Road (now A167) overbridge and no trace now remains. Around a mile north of the former station, the line crosses the River Wear on a dramatic viaduct. Langley Moor viaduct is crossed shortly afterwards and around a mile to the north, the line curves sharply to the right as it passes the site of the complex of junctions once known as Deerness Valley Junction; the site is also often referred to as Relly Mill or Stone Bridge (which is how it is shown on the OS map), named after the road overbridge.

Deerness Valley Junction was the point where lines from Bishop Auckland, Waterhouses and Consett joined the main line. The courses of these lines can clearly be seen and are now foot and cycle ways. The main line was realigned through this section in 1969 and again in 1974, following closure of the branch lines, to increase the line speed.

After Deerness Valley, the line curves to the right and crosses a viaduct before entering the deep cutting at Neville's Cross. Emerging from the cutting, the line starts to descend as it curves to the left before crossing Durham viaduct and enters the station.

This is one of the two highlights of the line and when travelling on trains, it is common to see passengers who had been blankly gazing out of the window, reading or using mobile telephones, to stop what they are doing and look out at the spectacular panorama below them, with Durham Cathedral and Castle dominating the scene.

Durham station is immediately to the north of the viaduct and is a mix of old and new. The station layout used to comprise two platforms and two through roads but the up through line was removed in 1972 when the tracks were realigned to increase the maximum permitted speed through the station. This particularly benefitted southbound trains as the line is on a rising gradient of 1 in 120 at this point, steepening to 1 in 101 before the summit at Relly Mill. In steam days, many southbound trains were banked out of the station as far as Relly Mill. The operational difficulties caused by this gradient were highlighted on 1 October 1994 when preserved A2 60532 *Blue Peter* stalled on the viaduct as it left Durham and in an attempt to restart the loco, the driver caused it to prime, causing the motion to 'run away' and resulting in serious damage to the locomotive's valve gear. The realignment of the tracks meant that the up platform canopy had to be replaced and its rather functional replacement survives to this day, in contrast to the original NER canopy on the Down platform.

As the train leaves Durham heading north, there is a final glimpse of the cathedral to the right. Around a mile to the north, the line curves to the left as it takes the 1970 Newton Hall deviation, which was built to avoid a sharp curve at the site of the former Newton Hall Junction (where the line to Sunderland diverged). The course of the original line can just be made out. The realignment allowed the line speed to be raised from 45 mph to 85 mph in this area.

The next station, Plawsworth, closed on 7 April 1952 and no trace remains. As the train heads north, the Penshaw Monument can be seen on the east side on the top of Penshaw Hill; this was built as a monument to the first Earl of Durham, one of the major coal mine owners at the time. The hill is immortalised in the local ballad *The Lambton Worm*. Another landmark, also visible on the east side, is the Lumley Castle Hotel.

Shortly afterwards, the train passes Chester-le-Street, where the station remains open. The station is unstaffed but for some years, an independent company called Chester-le-Track ran a ticket office-cum-travel agency from the station but this has now, sadly, closed after the company ceased trading in 2018. Just north of the station, the line crosses a high viaduct over the town and around a mile to the north we come to the site of Ouston Junction, where the Consett line converged from the west. This carried the Tyne Dock–Consett iron ore trains between 1966 and 1974; the steelworks closed in 1980. There are two local landmarks: the greyhound racing track and the Komatsu factory.

Birtley station (closed 5 December 1955) was just to the north and was located on a road bridge. The station has now been demolished but for many years, the derelict Station Inn reminded travellers that there was once a station here but this has also been demolished.

The double track now becomes four tracks as we approach Tyne Yard, which can be seen on the west side. If you are very quick, you will also see the trackbed of the Bowes Railway on the right at the point where it passed underneath the ECML, just before the disused yard flyover on the left. The flyover means that it is not always easy to see stock in the yard, especially if there are freight trains berthed in the adjacent sidings.

The works associated with the building of Tyne Yard mean that the former Lamesley station (closed 4 June 1945) has disappeared without trace; it was located approximately where the road bridge (Smithy Lane) at the north end of the yard now stands. This is a popular location for enthusiasts! The Angel of the North can be glimpsed on the right as the train continues its journey north, soon passing the site of Low Fell station (closed 7 April 1952), of which no trace remains; immediately to the north the connecting line to the Tyne Valley line diverges to the left and the short-lived Royal Mail terminal can be seen. The line is now running on an embankment which changes to a cutting at the approximate site of Bensham station (closed 5 April 1954) which has also disappeared without trace.

The Tyne Valley line crosses under the ECML and then rises to join it on the right as the train approaches King Edward Bridge South Junction, where the line curves sharply to the left to cross the Tyne via the King Edward Bridge; the line to the High Level Bridge and Sunderland diverges to the right.

The crossing of the Tyne is the second highlight of the journey, as we cross the historic boundary between Durham and Northumberland and journey's end at the spectacular Newcastle Central station, listed Grade I.

On 12 January 1992, the 0930 Edinburgh–Kings Cross crosses the Tees at Croft and leaves County Durham for Yorkshire.

On 19 February 1989, 20156 *HMS Endeavour* and 20122 *Cleveland Potash* are seen on the Darlington avoiding line on 6P62 Cemetery North–Thrislington lime empties. The 20s came off here and were replaced by 47301, which can be seen in the background behind the train.

On 19 February 1989, 31229 shunts a ballast train at Darlington.

On 25 May 1989, 47276 passes Darlington on the Immingham–Leith Norsk Hydro fertiliser train. The wires have yet to appear.

On 7 March 1990, instruction unit 935, formerly a class 302, is seen at Darlington. I believe this was the only slam-door EMU to be painted in InterCity livery.

The OLE structures have started to appear at Ferryhill on 27 November 1988 as 31215 approaches the station site on a southbound engineers' train.

On 14 May 1989, 31468 propels an engineers' train into Ferryhill yard. The station comprised an island platform with the entrance from the road bridge although subsequent track realignment and rebuilding of the bridge mean that there is now no trace of it at rail level.

A regular sight on the northern ECML for much of the early '90s was 5L82 Edinburgh–Cambridge empty parcels vans; as it also ran on a Saturday, it was popular with photographers. On a snowy 27 February 1993, 90016 approaches Tursdale Junction on this working. The now disused Leamside line is in the foreground.

An interesting working during the summer of 1990 was the 1021 Saturdays-only Skegness–Newcastle, which brought unusual traction, and (by this time) the rare experience of Mk 1 coaches to the North East. On 8 September 1990, 47344 crosses Croxdale viaduct on this working. On arrival at Newcastle, it went to Heaton and then returned south as ecs.

On 24 April 1994, 91024 passes the site of Croxdale station, of which no trace now remains, on the 0900 Kings Cross–Edinburgh. The station buildings were on the road bridge.

On 21 January 1989, class 101 S800 (recently transferred from the Western Region and still carrying first-class markings) stops at Durham on the 0826 Darlington–Newcastle, at that time one of only a handful of trains that stopped at Chester-le-Street.

On 23 May 1989, OLE structures have started to appear on Durham viaduct as 37071 crosses on 7S66 Tees–Stranraer Speedlink.

You could call this shot a double reverse as 91009 *The Samaritans* is blunt end first and coupled to a set in reverse formation! The set is seen leaving Durham on the 0900 Kings Cross–Glasgow Central on 15 March 1998.

On 10 January 1999, 56033 *Shotton Paper Mill* is seen on the Newton Hall deviation on a southbound mgr.

On 4 October 1997, 60007 *Sir Nigel Gresley* passes the site of Plawsworth station on Days Out's 'Flying Scotsman' tour from Kings Cross to Edinburgh Waverley.

On 7 April 2002, 47829, carrying its very eye-catching Police livery, approaches Plawsworth on the 1454 (Sundays) Newcastle–Birmingham New Street.

On 7 May 1989, 43173 is seen just south of Chester-le-Street on the 1345 (Sundays) Newcastle–Plymouth. Note that there is an extra TRSB in the formation, presumably being transferred for operational reasons. This viewpoint is no longer possible as houses have been built here.

On 7 May 1989, 47448 *Gateshead* crosses Chester-le-Street viaduct on the 1405 (Sundays) Newcastle–Liverpool Lime Street.

On 14 September 1996, 20305 and 20304 pass Chester-le-Street on 1Z58, the return leg of Pathfinder Tours' 'Geordie Chopper' tour from Bristol Temple Meads to Newcastle, which also did a circuit of the Tyne bridges hauled by 08633!

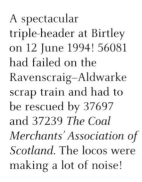

A spectacular triple-header at Birtley on 12 June 1994! 56081 had failed on the Ravenscraig–Aldwarke scrap train and had to be rescued by 37697 and 37239 *The Coal Merchants' Association of Scotland.* The locos were making a lot of noise!

On 11 March 2001, 47843 *Vulcan* approaches Birtley on the 1454 (Sundays) Newcastle–Bristol Temple Meads. The Angel of the North now dominates the skyline.

A reminder of the Regional Eurostar fiasco! As many readers will be aware, there were proposals to run so-called 'Regional Eurostars' from various parts of the UK through the Channel Tunnel to Paris. As part of this, sets 3308 and 3307 were dragged from North Pole to Polmadie by 37601 and 37606 on 3 June 1997 for staff familiarisation and are seen passing Tyne Yard. As is well known, these services never happened, mainly because the journey times would not be competitive against air and the growth of low-cost air travel. As far as I am aware, this was the only time a Eurostar set got to Tyneside or Scotland.

On 29 June 1989, 47102 approaches Low Fell on 6L97 Mossend–Ripple Lane Speedlink. Electrification works are not complete; note the return conductor looped around the top of the nearest OLE structure!

On 14 November 1992, an accident near Morpeth resulted in the Thornaby breakdown crane being called out and here we see 37104 taking it back home after the wreckage had been cleared from the site. Trains were diverted via the Blyth & Tyne and had I known that (no internet in those days) I would have gone there, but this photo was a reasonable consolation and remains the only photo I have of a breakdown crane on the move.

Class 90s only occasionally appeared north of York in passenger service as their lower maximum speed (110 mph in comparison to the 125 mph of a class 91) meant they could not keep time on the long non-stop runs. On 12 June 1994, though, 90024 did make an appearance on what I believe was the 1200 (Sundays) Kings Cross–Glasgow Central and is seen passing the site of Low Fell station. I have no way of knowing if the 90 worked through to Glasgow.

The mileage of this location is obvious! On 5 June 1993, 08886 scuttles north near the site of Bensham station, presumably en route from Tyne Yard to Heaton.

2

Darlington to Thornaby

Trains from Darlington towards Thornaby and Middlesbrough depart in a southerly direction before the Middlesbrough line turns to the east, away from the ECML, and takes up an easterly course. This section of line opened in 1887.

After leaving Darlington and passing the town's football stadium on the right, the line heads east through attractive countryside and soon passes Dinsdale station. Beyond Dinsdale, the line does a dog-leg and then joins the course of the former Stockton & Darlington Railway (opened in 1825) at the site of Oak Tree Junction. The nearby Fighting Cocks pub is famous as being the former booking office for the Stockton & Darlington Railway.

The line heads east and soon passes Teesside Airport station, now a Parliamentary station with one train a week on Sundays only. The station opened on 3 October 1971 but usage was never high because it is around a mile from the airport. As the only train that now calls is a westbound one, the eastbound (Down) platform and footbridge were taken out of use in December 2017; one unfortunate consequence was the loss of a very good photographic location from the footbridge!

The airport itself, now known as Teesside International Airport after a period of being known as Durham Tees Valley Airport, was originally the RAF Bomber Command station of Middleton St George and Lancasters and Halifaxes of Number 6 (Royal Canadian Air Force) Group were stationed here during the Second World War. One of the Canadian squadrons based here was number 419, nicknamed the Moose' squadron. The most famous member of this squadron was Pilot Officer Andrew Charles Mynarski, who was posthumously awarded the Victoria Cross when he attempted, sadly unsuccessfully, to save the life of the tail gunner of his Lancaster after it had been attacked and set on fire in a raid on 12 June 1944. A statue of him was erected outside the former Officers' Mess (later the St George Hotel) in 2005.

Middleton St George closed as an RAF base in 1964 and opened as a civilian airport two years later.

The line continues eastwards and soon passes Urlay Nook level crossing, which was controlled by a signal box, although that was decommissioned in 2019. Shortly afterwards, Allen's West station is reached, which was built to serve a local munitions factory during the Second World War and did not become a public station until 3 October 1971. Significant housing development has taken place around the station in recent years.

The line then curves to the left and just before Eaglescliffe station, the Leeds Northern line from Northallerton trails in on the left. Eaglescliffe station is immediately north of the junction and the line is now running in an approximately south-west to north-easterly direction. Eaglescliffe now has a single island platform; there was a second to the west but this was taken out of use and demolished in the late 1960s. The station was unstaffed for many years but in 2012, Chester-le-Track opened a ticket office here. This closed after the company ceased trading in 2018 but has since reopened, run by Northern and Grand Central, whose London to Sunderland expresses now stop here.

Immediately to the north of the station is a footpath bridge known to local enthusiasts as 'dog muck bridge' because of its popularity with dog walkers. Although a good photographic location, it is wise to watch where you step!

The line continues in a north-easterly direction. This section was originally four tracks and the wide formation remains obvious. Just over a mile after leaving Eaglescliffe, the line turns to the east at Stockton Cut Junction as the Durham Coast line continues straight on. The line then joins the north to east spur from the Durham Coast line at Bowesfield Junction and passed Bowesfield signal box, which was on the right until it was decommissioned in 2019, then running parallel to the A66 trunk road for a short distance as both cross the Tees into the former North Riding of Yorkshire. Shortly afterwards, the line passes under a series of overbridges and arrives at Thornaby station, where this part of our journey ends. The station comprises a single island platform and like Eaglescliffe, was unstaffed for many years. The once attractive station building was demolished in 1981, making the station a rather exposed and windswept place, although a new ticket office in brick chalet style was opened in 2003.

The station is popular with enthusiasts as it overlooks the west end of the former Tees Yard, although rail freight activity in this area is much reduced from the 1980s and '90s.

On 4 February 1995, flooding at Yarm meant that trains were diverted via and reversed at Darlington. Here we see 60020 *Great Whernside* passing Dinsdale on what was possibly 6N39 Leeds–Port Clarence empties.

On 12 April 1998, ECML trains were diverted via the coast between Darlington and Newcastle. Here we see 47733 *Eastern Star* and 82214 at Middleton, just west of Teesside Airport, on the 1200 Kings Cross–Glasgow Central.

On 12 April 1998, trains were diverted via Dinsdale and the coast owing to a possession on the ECML. Here we see 43108 passing Teesside Airport on the diverted 1100 Kings Cross–Aberdeen.

On 11 June 1987, a 101 arrives at Eaglescliffe on the 1242 Hartlepool–Darlington.

On 8 July 1996, 56031 heads north at Eaglescliffe on 6E65 Glazebrook–Haverton Hill petrol empties. The space occupied by the now demolished second island platform can be seen in the right background.

On 8 July 1996, 56134 *Blyth Power* and 56061 unusually double-head 4L79 Wilton–Felixstowe Freightliner as they approach Eaglescliffe. The former four-track formation is clearly visible.

On 30 March 1997, 47737 *Resurgent* drags 91003 away from Eaglescliffe on the diverted 0945 (Sundays) Doncaster–Glasgow Central. The infamous 'dog muck bridge' can be seen in the background.

On 16 August 1997, 47750 *Royal Mail Cheltenham* approaches Eaglescliffe on an excursion from Durham via the coast to Carlisle, returning via the S&C.

3

Durham Coast Line and the Stillington Branch

We retrace our steps from Thornaby station towards Bowesfield Junction, where the Durham Coast line takes a right-hand curve to join the line from Stockton Cut Junction at Hartburn Junction. The line from Stockton Cut Junction and Eaglescliffe only saw passenger services on Sundays for many years, namely a Parliamentary service from Darlington to Hartlepool. This had run daily until the service cuts of 1991, when it was reduced to a minimal service on Sunday afternoons only; at present there are two return trips. Usage of the spur increased with the introduction of Grand Central services from Sunderland to Kings Cross in 2007.

The line heads northwards from Hartburn Junction towards Stockton station, passing the scrapyard of TJ Thomson on the west side, which is still rail served. Stockton station itself has seen much better days; it once had an arched overall roof, which was removed in 1978, as well as goods lines running to the west of the station. After the roof had been removed, the station became derelict and was reduced to an unstaffed halt in late 1988. At this time, a visitor could have been forgiven for thinking the station was closed; it looked so uninviting and one wonders how many potential passengers were discouraged from using it out of fears for their personal safety.

Matters started to improve in the early 1990s when the building was refurbished for a new lease of life as a care home and a footbridge was built to replace the very uninviting subway between the platforms. In addition, the derelict bay platforms at the northern end of the station were filled in and the site generally tidied up.

The area north of the station once encompassed a large yard, much of which has now been built over. In addition, the railway itself was realigned north of the station in 1993 to accommodate a new road scheme.

Leaving Stockton behind, the railway now heads in a north-westerly direction for around 2 miles until Norton South Junction is reached. This was one of the last triangular junctions remaining which had a manual signal box controlling each of the three junctions. Trains for the Durham Coast line turn right at Norton South Junction. The line to Norton West and on to Ferryhill is freight-only, although at one time was a regular diversionary route off the ECML; it is still occasionally used as such.

The line turns through around 120 degrees before reaching Norton East box (which is listed Grade II), the third of the triangle, and usually switched out. The third side of the triangle now sees little use although at one time the Cemetery North (Hartlepool)–Ferryhill lime trains used it daily, sometimes even on Sundays.

The line now heads towards the east and around half a mile beyond Norton East box, passes the site of Norton-on-Tees station (closed 7 March 1960) and its very tall signal box, which has now been decommissioned, before crossing the A19 road and the site of the original Billingham station (closed after the last trains on 6 November 1966 with the new station opening the next day); there was a tall NER signal box and there also remains a traditional NER footbridge at the adjacent level crossing. The line serving the remains of the chemical industry on Teesside heads straight at the junction, while the coast line then turns to head in a north-easterly direction and passes the new and very austere Billingham station. This was originally provided with a ticket office (still visible) but this was closed in 1969.

Belasis Lane signal box was around a mile from Billingham Junction on the freight line, which divides here to serve the various industrial sites. The area was still busy with rail freight until the early 2000s but has declined significantly since then. Much of the network sees little or no use at present and the line to Seal Sands was taken out of use following the Durham Coast resignalling.

The main line continues in a north-easterly direction from Billingham new station and leaving the town behind, passes the Cowpen Bewley Woodland Country Park on the right before reaching the closed Greatham station. The signal box and platforms still survived here; the station itself closed as late as 25 November 1991 although usage had been very light for many years previously as the village (around ¾ mile to the north) was much better served by local buses.

Greatham signal box was the last to be passed until Ryhope Grange Junction as the line north of here was resignalled in the early 2010s. The remaining section to the south was resignalled in early 2021. Belasis Lane box was decommissioned on 23 January and Norton South, Norton East, Norton-on-Tees, Billingham, Greatham and Ryhope Grange Junction followed on 6 February. This significantly reduced the number of surviving North Eastern Railway signal boxes.

Beyond Greatham, the line starts to curve to head in a more northerly direction and on the east side, the branch from Hartlepool nuclear power station trails in at Seaton Snook Junction. Seaton Carew station is just to the north; the very austere station is not a particularly good advertisement for the seaside town it serves.

Heading north, the line passes through the derelict Cliff House yards, and it is difficult to imagine just how industrialised this area once was. The line then passes the southern outskirts of Hartlepool, with the sea briefly visible on the east side of the line, before the line turns west and inland at Newburn (this was the site of West Hartlepool steam shed). Hartlepool station is half a mile or so beyond. At this point the line has turned through 90 degrees and 'northbound' trains are briefly heading west as they pass through the station, which is on a sharp right-hand curve.

Hartlepool station and its surrounding area has seen many changes. A peculiar feature of the station is that the Up (southbound) platform has been disused for many years (it is believed since the mid to late 1960s) and all passenger trains use the reversible Down platform, although the Up line is still used by southbound freights. The area immediately east and north of the station, between it and the sea, was once industrial but has now been redeveloped as a retail park and marina and a new road crosses the railway at the 'north' (actually west) end of the station; the platform was shortened in around 1995 to accommodate this. Most of the semaphores at this station were replaced in 1987, before the rest of the line was resignalled.

Hartlepool originally consisted of two separate towns. The original town was on a headland to the east, which can be seen as the train heads north from the station but this was overshadowed by the Victorian industrial town that for many years was known as West Hartlepool, until the two towns were merged in 1967. The town is probably best known for the apocryphal tale that during the Napoleonic Wars, a monkey is alleged to have been the only survivor from a French warship that foundered off the coast of the town and the locals, having seen neither a monkey nor a Frenchman before, accused it of being a French spy, put it on trial and hanged it, leading to the 'Monkeyhangers' nickname being bestowed on the town's inhabitants ever since!

As a result, the town's football club's mascot is called H'angus the Monkey and in a bizarre twist, the man who regularly wore it at home matches, Stuart Drummond, stood for election as mayor of Hartlepool in 2002 as an independent under the name 'H'angus the Monkey', on a platform including free bananas for schoolchildren. He not only won but was re-elected in 2005 and 2009, stepping down when his term ended in 2013 after the town voted to abolish the office of elected mayor.

As the train leaves Hartlepool, the line takes another 90-degree bend and heads north; on the west side the site of Hartlepool FC's former stadium, the Victoria Ground, can be seen and on the east, there are views of the new marina and retail development, with the headland and 'old' Hartlepool visible in the background. A line diverges into the docks at this point (Lancaster Road Junction) and the line then takes a sharp left-hand curve to head in a north-westerly direction, passing the site of Cemetery North Junction and signal box as well as the former Steetley works. At this point the line from old Hartlepool formed a triangular junction on the east side of the line; services on this line ceased on 16 June 1947.

Beyond Cemetery North, the line is now on an embankment and there are views of the North Sea on the east side. Around two miles beyond the line passes the site of Hart station (closed 31 August 1953), marked by a footbridge, and then turns northwards along the newest section of the line, opened by the North Eastern Railway in 1905 to avoid the original inland route with its 1 in 39 bank at Seaton, south of Sunderland. The course of the original line can be seen on the west side, taking a straight line, and is now a cycle way. It closed to passengers on 9 June 1952 but remained open for freight for many years afterwards.

Just to the north, the line crosses Crimdon Dene viaduct, one of the major engineering features of the line, and then follows the coast through the site of Blackhall Rocks (closed 4 January 1960) and Blackhall Colliery (closed 4 May 1964) stations, before crossing Castle Eden Dene viaduct ('dene' is a North East term for a wooded river valley) and passing the site of Horden station (closed 6 September 1965). A new station, called Horden Peterlee, opened on 29 June 2020, just north of the former station site. Peterlee was designated as a New Town in 1948 and is unusual in that it is named after an individual – Peter Lee was a Durham miners' leader, local councillor and Methodist preacher who died in 1935. Unfortunately, the town was built west of the railway and Horden station and is also smaller than many of the other New Towns in the area, with a population of around 20,000.

As such, it could not save Horden station from closure but it is hoped the new station will be more successful than its predecessor.

This area is former coal mining country but little trace now remains; Horden Colliery (closed 1987) was on the west side of the line just north of the location of the new station. As the line heads north, it passes Easington (station closed 4 May 1964), whose colliery was one of the last to close in County Durham, surviving until 1993. It was also on the west side of the line and no trace remains. The signal box survived after the closure of the station to control the junction for the colliery branch until that closed.

The line continues to head north in close proximity to the sea and crosses another viaduct at Hawthorn Dene before entering the town of Seaham. The history of the railways of Seaham and south Sunderland is complex. The line from Sunderland to Seaham was originally owned by the Londonderry Railway, built by the Marquess of Londonderry, who also owned the coal mines in the area and built the town. The Seaham–Sunderland section was bought out by the North Eastern Railway in 1900. As the train approaches Seaham, the line from the docks (now serving a cement terminal) trails in on the east side. Dawdon Colliery was also located in this area on the west side of the line but no trace remains.

Just before the train arrives at Seaham, the branch from Seaham Colliery trailed in on the west side; the mine closed in 1992. It had previously been merged with the nearby Vane Tempest Colliery. Seaham station has been reduced to an unstaffed halt and the NER signal box that once dominated the scene was decommissioned when the line was resignalled. The present Seaham station dates from the opening of the line to Hart in 1905. It replaced the Londonderry Railway station which has now been demolished.

Leaving Seaham, the train heads north and then proceeds through a series of reverse curves as it passes Hall Dene level crossing, once the location of the private station serving the Londonderrys' residence at Seaham Hall, as well as the connections to Vane Tempest Colliery before it merged with Seaham Colliery. The line then runs on a clifftop with the North Sea visible on the east side and then approaches the site of Ryhope East station (closed 7 March 1960), of which no trace remains. Almost immediately to the north, the original NER line from Hart via Seaton trailed in on the west side. A section remained open to serve Murton Colliery until 1989 and there was a separate station at Ryhope on this line. The characteristic NER cast-iron footbridge remained until the tracks were lifted in the early 1990s.

Ryhope (pronounced 'rye-up') also has a connection with Bomber Command: on 31 March 1944 Cyril Joe Barton, a Halifax pilot with 578 Squadron, was awarded a posthumous VC after pressing on to attack the target after his Halifax bomber was badly damaged in the notorious Nuremberg raid (when the RAF lost 95 aircraft from a total of 795). On the return journey his aircraft had started to run out of fuel as it approached the coast at Ryhope and almost his last act before the aircraft crash-landed was to steer it away from a row of terraced houses. Tragically, as well as Barton, one person in the village was killed.

The line now passes a series of sidings, now much reduced in importance, as it passed Ryhope Grange Junction signal box, of traditional NER design, on the west side of the line. A freight-only line serving Ryhope and Silksworth collieries also diverged inland at this point – much of this is now a footway. The line then turns inland at the point where the branch to Sunderland South Dock diverges. This heads almost due north as the line to Sunderland takes a more north-westerly route.

A new road has recently been built in the area, which crosses the railway close to the junction.

The South Dock branch presently sees little use but until the early 1980s it was relatively busy with coal traffic; there was a steam shed and latterly a diesel depot at South Dock which closed in 1991 as a consequence of the decline of the coal industry. Most of the coal traffic was diverted to the new Tyne Coal Terminal when that opened in 1985 as it could handle larger ships than South Dock. By the early 1990s, the only regular traffic was a daily train of petroleum products from Petrofina's refinery at Immingham to a delivery terminal in the docks. This ceased in the early 2000s.

From Ryhope Grange Junction, the South Dock line runs close to the sea in an almost straight line for around three-quarters of a mile until the site of the former Hendon yards is reached. At this point Hendon Junction signal box controlled the junction for the steeply graded branch down to the docks themselves, as well as the former connecting line towards Fawcett Street Junction in Sunderland, where it joined the former line from Sunderland to Durham, part of which was reopened for Tyne & Wear Metro trains on 31 March 2002. Hendon was the site of the original station of the Londonderry Railway which was replaced by the present Sunderland Central station in 1879.

The steepness of the gradient from Hendon to the docks meant that the Petrofina train had to be worked in two sections downhill from Hendon.

Back on the main line, the train passes through the two Sunderland South Tunnels (which passed under the Hendon–Fawcett Street Junction line) before emerging at Sunderland South Junction – the electrified line from South Hylton used by Tyne & Wear Metro trains converges from the west side. This area had been used as siding accommodation after the closure of the line to Durham in 1964. The Durham & Sunderland Railway's Fawcett Street station was just to the east of here and a commemorative plaque in a retaining wall in the parallel street marks the spot.

The line then plunges into a covered way. Sunderland station is located in this covered way and consists of a single island platform, sub-divided into two on each side to allow heavy rail and Metro trains to use the same platform.

Before the Sunderland Direct project brought Metro trains to Sunderland, the station was located in a cutting and daylight did reach its island platform, a scene that seems difficult to imagine today. Sunderland station (originally known as Sunderland Central to distinguish it from Hendon, Fawcett Street and Monkwearmouth stations) originally comprised two island platforms and an overall roof, but the roof was destroyed in an air raid in 1942. The roof was replaced by individual canopies after the war and the station was rationalised to a single island platform (the easternmost) in the 1960s, with the other used for parcels traffic until this ceased in the mid-1980s.

Returning back to Norton South Junction, trains towards Ferryhill would take the west curve at Norton South Junction. At Norton West Junction, where there was a signal box and level crossing, the little-used curve from Norton East trails in on the east side. This line is still occasionally used as a diversionary route but less often than in the past; there are still long-term aspirations to introduce a Newcastle–Middlesbrough express service by this route but at the time of writing, the uncertainty over traffic levels as a result of the Covid-19 crisis means that this may not happen for some time. Passenger services had ceased on 31 March 1952.

After Norton West Junction, the line then heads east and passed under the long-closed Thornaby–Sunderland via Wynyard line at Redmarshall. There were north-east and west-south curves here and as a result, Redmarshall was one of the few places to have junctions named after all four points of the compass.

The Redmarshall South to West curve trailed in on the south side of the line and from here to Stillington Junction, around 5 miles to the west, the line was quadruple track, with the southern pair of lines being electrified at 1500 V DC overhead between 1915 and 1935 as part of the North Eastern Railway's Shildon–Newport electrification scheme. The formation is clearly still wide enough for four tracks.

Carlton station, renamed Redmarshall after the Grouping as part of a scheme by the LNER to minimise confusion between stations in different areas with the same name, was just west of the junction and consisted of an island platform on the non-electrified lines only; access was from a road bridge.

Beyond, the line continues eastwards until Stillington station site is reached. This also consisted of an island platform on the northern non-electrified pair of tracks. The signal box here survived until the mid-1990s although was usually switched out in its latter years. Stillington Junction was around half a mile to the west and at this point, the once electrified line to Shildon diverged and the line to Ferryhill turned towards the north, before passing the site of Sedgefield station. Little trace remains at platform level although the street-level ticket office (complete with characteristic NER cast-iron grilled window) remained into the 2000s. The station was around 1 ½ miles west of the small town it purported to serve and as a result, buses had taken most of its traffic long before it closed. The town became famous in the late '90s as it was the constituency of the then Prime Minister, Tony Blair.

Beyond Sedgefield, the line heads north for around a mile and then turns to the west to join the ECML at Ferryhill. A feature of this section, which can also be seen from the ECML, is a large LNER cut-out lineside sign on the Up side reading 'Stockton'.

On 30 October 1988, 47475 passes Stockton, before it was renovated, on the diverted 1130 Newcastle–Liverpool Lime Street.

On 16 June 1989, 37069 approaches Stockton on a southbound train of Ferrywagons, before the line was re-routed north of the station. The footbridge in the background has been replaced with a modern example and the gasometer has been demolished.

On 15 June 1996, 60020 *Great Whernside* approaches Stockton on 6M46 Redcar–Hardendale limestone empties.

On 30 March 1997, 47766 *Resolute* drags 91025 past Stockton on the diverted 0900 (Sundays) York–Glasgow Central. The area had been tidied up significantly by this time and the tracks had been realigned as part of a local road scheme.

Another 30 March 1997 diversion as 43014 approaches Stockton on the diverted 0950 Newcastle–Plymouth. This power car is now part of the New Measurement Train.

On 30 October 1988, 43065 approaches Norton West Junction on the diverted 1015 (Sundays) Newcastle–Kings Cross. This power car was later used by Grand Central and re-engined and renumbered 43465. It was subsequently used by East Midlands Trains and East Midlands Railway, although it went off-lease at the end of 2020.

The footbridge at Norton is taller than usual and gives excellent views of the line. On 15 March 2003, 60097 *Port of Grimsby and Immingham* approaches the station site on 6M46 Redcar–Hardendale limestone empties, diverted via the coast owing to a possession on the ECML.

On 15 March 2003, 142095 passes Norton on the 1036 Carlisle–Middlesbrough. One pities the poor passengers who were forced to make the complete journey!

On 12 April 1998 ECML services were diverted via the coast owing to a possession at Tursdale and here we see 43194 passing the site of Billingham old station on the diverted 1014 (Sundays) Edinburgh–Penzance.

In the early part of 2003, some Trans-Pennine services were diverted via the coast line at weekends and on 15 March 2003, 158743 passes the site of Billingham old station on the 1250 Newcastle–Liverpool Lime Street. Note that the semaphore junction signal had been replaced by two single posts since 1998. Also note that the pub still carries the name 'The Station' over thirty-six years after relocation!

On 18 October 1989, 37046 is seen on the Port Clarence branch as it approaches Billingham on 6O49 Haverton Hill–Eastleigh Speedlink. Belasis Lane signal box is in the distance.

Belasis Lane signal box was around a mile north of the junction at Billingham and was in a very industrial setting; very few railtours ever visit the line. One exception was the BLS 'Durham Coast Railtour', reporting number 1Z39, which ran from Linlithgow on 12 August 2000 and visited Seal Sands, Seaton-on-Tees, Hartlepool Docks and Sunderland South Dock. Here we see the driver of 37428 surrendering the token for the Seal Sands branch to the signaller. 37415 was at the rear of the train. The box has been decommissioned and the line carries far less traffic than previously.

Greatham station closed on 25 November 1991 although the last trains called on Saturday 23 November. On that day 156438 passes on the 1100 Middlesbrough–Newcastle.

Another view of the BLS 'Durham Coast Railtour' from Linlithgow, seen heading for Hartlepool nuclear power station. 37428 leads with 37415 at the rear.

Class 26s were never a common sight in north-east England, or indeed anywhere outside Scotland. On 13 March 1993, 26003 and 26005 made a rare trip south of the border on Victoria Travel's 'The Cumbrian Tynesider' from Manchester Victoria via the S&C to Carlisle and thence via Newcastle, the Durham Coast, York, the Calder Valley, Manchester Victoria, Carlisle and back to Manchester! The 26s worked the tour on the Carlisle–Carlisle leg and are seen at Newburn, south of Hartlepool.

The semaphores at the south (actually east) end of Hartlepool station are on borrowed time on 11 June 1987 as 143018 arrives on the 1503 Middlesbrough–Newcastle. The masts in the background remind us that HMS *Warrior*, now at Portsmouth, was restored to her present condition in Hartlepool.

On 5 May 1990, we see 47219, carrying the unofficial name *Sandpiper*, at the disused Up platform at Hartlepool on 1Z15, the BLS 'Tyne Tees Wanderer' from Birmingham New Street to various freight lines in the North East in a day of typically thick coastal fog (known locally as 'sea fret')! The leading engine, 47375 *Tinsley Traction Depot – Quality Approved*, is out of sight at the front of the train; 47219 was attached here. Attitudes were a bit more laid-back about taking photos from the track in those days! The new road bridge now crosses the line at this point.

On 13 March 1993, 56118 passes Hartlepool on northbound mgr empties.

Taken from the new road bridge, we see 56109 passing Hartlepool on 1Z46, Hertfordshire Railtours' 'East Coast Diversion' tour from Kings Cross to Newcastle on 17 January 1998. The derelict area behind the station has now been redeveloped as a retail and leisure park. The shortened platform is evident.

On 12 April 1998, 47772 drags 91030 on the approach to Hartlepool on the diverted 1500 Edinburgh–Kings Cross. This was also taken from the new road bridge, which offers a number of photographic opportunities. Clarence Road box and the Victoria Ground can be seen in the background.

On 27 May 1995, 60024 *Elizabeth Fry* approaches Hart on 6D40 Sunderland South Dock–Lindsey empty petrol tanks. The course of the original inland route can be seen on the left.

On 27 May 1995, D172 *Ixion* passes Hart on 1Z46, Pathfinder Tours' 'Severn Tyne Express' from Bristol Temple Meads to Newcastle (despite the headcode!). The train then returned south via the ECML.

On a bitterly cold 23 November 1996, 60532 *Blue Peter* and 47971 *Robin Hood* pass the site of Hart station on the SRPS 'North Briton' tour from York to Carlisle and back to York. *Blue Peter* came on at Middlesbrough and worked through to Carlisle and thence to Preston. The tour was around 2 ½ hours late at this point and in the days before mobile telephones and Real Time Trains, no one knew if it was running or not. The Steetley works can be seen in the distance.

On 12 April 1998, Easter Sunday, 47772 drags 91023 across Crimdon Dene viaduct on the diverted 0930 Newcastle–Kings Cross.

On 3 July 1989, 56126 passes Horden signal box on a southbound mgr. The box was closed a few months later. The new Horden Peterlee station is located towards the rear of the train and the former colliery was located in the left background – it had been demolished by this time.

Also on 3 July 1989, 31205 and 31299 head north past Easington to work 6D40 South Dock–Lindsey petrol empties. The signal box can be seen on the left.

On 29 March 2003, 37707 and 37684 are seen at Dawdon, south of Seaham, on 1Z56, the return working of Pathfinder Tours' 'Tyne Line' railtour from Derby to Newcastle. The 37s worked from Newcastle to Doncaster.

On 16 June 1989, 56120 passes Seaham on mgr empties from the Tyne Coal Terminal to Seaham Colliery. This was taken from the signal box by invitation.

On 16 June 1989, 56120 (also seen in the previous photo) takes the branch to Seaham Colliery.

On 22 July 1992, 156463 passes Seaham signal box on the 1648 Nunthorpe–Newcastle.

On 17 September 1988, 47413 heads south at Ryhope on the 1710 Newcastle–Middlesbrough Pacer replacer. This was regularly loco-hauled that summer.

On 27 March 1993, 56129 (front) and 56116 (rear) take the Murton branch at Ryhope, passing the site of Ryhope station, on 1Z37, Pathfinder Tours' 'Tyne Tees Trekker' from Bristol Temple Meads, which also visited Tyne Dock, Jarrow and Seal Sands. This was the last railtour to Murton and the only train I ever photographed on the branch.

On 9 September 1990, 47533 and 47474 *Sir Rowland Hill* take the South Dock branch at Ryhope Grange Junction on 1Z30, the BLS 'Tyne Tees Wanderer II' tour from Manchester to the North East. The tour visited Raisby Hill and the Leamside line – a photo on the former line can be found in chapter 8. A new road bridge now crosses the line at around this point.

On 9 July 1996, 20902 (with 20903 at the other end) are seen approaching Ryhope Grange Junction on a weedkilling train, which had visited South Dock. The line was unfenced, so photography was relatively easy. A new road bridge crosses the line here, as also mentioned in the caption for the previous photo.

On a very dull 27 November 1993, 56094 *Eggborough Power Station* is seen at the Petrofina terminal at Sunderland South Dock as it shunts the wagons to form 6D40 petrol empties to Lindsey. This was the only time I ever saw a 56 on this working and typically the weather was foul! This was within the docks area; I had been allowed in by a friendly gate warden.

The classic view of the Petrofina terminal at South Dock, taken in rather better weather, as we see 60003 *Christopher Wren* in the terminal on 19 February 1994. This was taken over a fence at the end of the cul-de-sac that led to the locomotive depot. At this time, the area had an unsavoury reputation and it was not wise to be seen carrying expensive cameras or to leave one's car unattended for any length of time.

On 17 August 1997, an accident exercise took place on the South Dock branch, simulating a van having been hit by a train. 37040 obliged and is seen following completion of the exercise. I doubt a nuclear flask wagon had ever been seen on the branch before!

On 30 October 1988, 47535 *University of Leicester* approaches the site of Redmarshall station on the diverted 0955 (Sundays) Newcastle–Poole. The formation on the left was once occupied by the slow lines, which were electrified between 1915 and 1935 as part of the NER's Shildon–Newport electrification scheme.

On 30 March 1997, 47788 *Captain Peter Mainsty* drags 91020 past the site of Redmarshall station on the diverted 1400 (Sundays) Kings Cross–Glasgow Central. The station consisted of an island platform between the tracks and has disappeared without trace. The formerly electrified slow lines were on the right.

On 5 May 1990, 47475, sporting its unique Regional Railways livery, passes the site of Stillington station on the diverted 1004 (Sundays) Newcastle–Liverpool Lime Street.

On a snowy 27 November 1988, 47422 passes the site of Sedgefield station on the diverted 0940 (Sundays) Newcastle–Liverpool Lime Street.

4

Leamside Line

The Leamside line was the original main line from Tyneside to the south until the present route via Durham and the Team Valley opened in 1872. After this, it became something of a backwater as far as passenger services were concerned but remained an important route for coal traffic well into the 1970s and early 1980s, as well as a diversionary route from the ECML. Its swansong was to be used between 11 and 19 March 1989 when the ECML was blocked at Durham for electrification work. It was mothballed in 1991 after the final diversions on 14 April and the last train to cover the entire line ran on 23 June 1993, worked by 37519; the line was not officially closed until 2012. The tracks have now been lifted but hope remains that a service may be restored between Newcastle and Washington.

Passenger services on the line were complex as a number of different overlapping services used it. Services over the southern section of the line ceased on 28 July 1941 when the service between Leamside and Ferryhill was withdrawn and after that the two main passenger services were Durham–Sunderland (using the line between Leamside and Penshaw) and Fencehouses–Newcastle.

The line starts at Tursdale Junction and its history as being the first line in the area is obvious as it takes a straight route whereas the present ECML diverges to the west. The line continued in a northwards direction for around 2 miles before turning to take a more north-easterly direction. Shincliffe station (closed 28 July 1941) was just south of an overbridge carrying the A177 road and the buildings remained in use as a pub and restaurant for many years.

Around half a mile to the north, the line crossed the A1(M) motorway (the bridge still remains); Whitwell signal box and level crossing were just to the north. The box has now been demolished but was a prominent landmark for drivers on the motorway for many years. The line then continued in a north-easterly direction before turning northwards again and passing the site of Sherburn Colliery station (closed 28 July 1941), which was immediately south of an overbridge carrying the B1283 road.

The line then continued in a largely northerly direction, skirting the eastern outskirts of Durham at Belmont (with tantalising glimpses of Durham Cathedral) and then crossed the A690 Durham to Sunderland road. Just to the north of this bridge was the site of Belmont Junction, where the freight-only line from Durham Belmont Goods station (also, briefly,

Gilesgate passenger station) trailed in on the west side, followed almost immediately by the site of Leamside Junction, where the line from Newton Hall Junction joined, which was used by trains from Durham to Sunderland until they were withdrawn on 4 May 1964.

Leamside station was around half a mile to the north, immediately south of the bridge carrying Station Road. Leamside is a very small community and the station was midway between Leamside and the larger community of Rainton Gate. It consisted of an island platform with bays at each end and was closed on 5 October 1953, although it opened as required on Sundays after that date until around 1958 when main line trains were diverted this way to allow passengers for Durham to change here. The station was subsequently demolished and the tracks realigned over its site, so no trace remains.

The line continued in a broadly northerly direction and a passenger in a forward-facing seat on the east side of a northbound train would see Penshaw Hill and the famous monument for the first time. As the line approached Fencehouses, large tracts of derelict land on either side of the line were evidence of the once extensive colliery workings in the area. A description of these is outside the scope of this book but there is much material available in print or online about the colliery railways of this area.

Fencehouses station was around 2 ½ miles north of Leamside and immediately north of a level crossing carrying the A1052 road. It was of the standard two-platform layout. By the 1980s, all traces of the station had disappeared but the NER signal box remained in use until the mothballing of the line in 1991. This was on the Up side of the line immediately south of the level crossing.

Still heading north, the line crossed over the A182 trunk road and the site of Penshaw station was just to the north. From Fencehouses, the line had been quadruple track with the western pair of lines used by passenger trains. Penshaw (pronounced 'Pensher') was an island platform just south of an underbridge carrying Station Road and was on the west side of the community it was named after – no trace now remains at rail level. At this point, a knowledgeable passenger would have tried to be sitting in a forward-facing seat on the west side of the train as the line approached the line's major landmark, the Victoria viaduct over the River Wear.

Immediately south of the viaduct was Penshaw North Junction. At this point the line was running in a north-easterly direction and trains for Sunderland would continue straight on until they were withdrawn on 4 May 1964 (freight continued until 21 August 1967). The Leamside line took a sharp curve to the west to head in a north-westerly direction over the Victoria viaduct, with spectacular views over the River Wear on both sides with a view of Penshaw Hill and Monument on the north side, before taking another sharp curve to reach the site of Washington South Junction and Washington station.

The bridge was completed on 28 June 1838, the date of the coronation of Queen Victoria – hence its name. It remains a spectacular landmark in the area and is around 120 feet above high water. It is listed Grade II*.

At Washington South Junction, the former Stanhope & Tyne Railway trailed in from the west. In its latter years, this line was the route of the famous Tyne Dock to Consett iron ore trains and is now a footpath-cum-cycleway. The S&T line closed in 1966 when the iron ore trains were re-routed via Gateshead but the section from Washington South

Junction towards Consett reopened in 1974, when the iron ore trains were diverted to Teesport. From then until the works closed in 1980, they travelled via Stillington and the Leamside line to reverse at Washington South Junction before heading to Consett. Washington station was immediately north of the junction and by the 1980s, only the former goods shed and a fragment of the Down platform remained as clues to its existence. The station was around three-quarters of a mile from the village it was named after, which is also the site of Washington Old Hall. This was the ancestral home of the Washington family, whose most famous member led the American War of Independence.

Once a small mining community, Washington was designated as a New Town in 1964 and now has a population of 67,000. A curious feature of the town is that it is divided into fifteen Districts which for many years were both named and numbered. The numbers were shown on the road signs in the town but these have now been replaced with the district names, many of which have an American flavour, such as Albany and Columbia. The designation of a New Town was too late to save the railway as the station had closed on 9 September 1963 when the (by then very limited) service from Washington to Newcastle, consisting of one Up train in the morning and one Down in the evening, was withdrawn. These had been timed for the benefit of workers at a nearby factory and the service has the dubious distinction of being the only one identified for closure in the Beeching Report for which no objections were received.

Washington North Junction was just north of the station, where the Stanhope & Tyne line diverged towards Tyne Dock. The line then headed north and passed under the A1231 Washington Highway heading in a largely northerly direction – Usworth station was around half a mile to the north and was located immediately south of a level crossing; the signal box remained here until the closure of the line. Like Washington, the station closed on 9 September 1963 and hardly any trace remains. During the Second World War, the station was busy with personnel travelling to and from the nearby RAF Usworth airbase. Much of the site of the airbase is now occupied by the Nissan car factory; the North East Land, Sea and Air Museum also occupies a small part of the site.

The line continued north, leaving Washington behind, through a short section of open country before the site of Follingsby Lane level crossing, followed by Wardley NCB exchange sidings and shed. There were a number of collieries in this area and a line remained open to the north until the early 1980s to serve a coking plant at Monkton. All NCB lines in the area had closed by the early 1980s. BR opened a Freightliner terminal here in 1967 but it closed in 1987. The site lay derelict for a few years and was then reused for the Wardley Coal Disposal Point, which opened in 1989, where coal from nearby opencast sites would be loaded onto MGR wagons. As such, the northern section of line remained open after the rest of the line closed. Wardley Disposal Point closed in around 2001 and the line became disused.

This section of line was also used to stable the Royal Train overnight on the night of 30 November–1 December 1990 when HM The Queen visited the North East.

The line then passed under the junction of the A194 and A184 highways before turning west and joining the line from Sunderland at Pelaw Junction, passing under the Metro line from South Shields as it did so.

On 11 March 1989, the first day of the eight-day Durham blockade, 43077 passes the site of Shincliffe station (at that time a restaurant) on the 0900 Kings Cross–Edinburgh.

On 29 October 1989, 47558 approaches the site of Sherburn Colliery station on the diverted 1009 (Sun) Newcastle–Liverpool Lime Street.

On 26 October 1989, 31315 passes the site of Sherburn Colliery station on an electrification train, just after 47558 and the 1009 Newcastle–Liverpool Lime Street had passed!

On 29 October 1989, 43108 passes the site of Leamside station on the diverted 0735 (Sun) Leeds–Glasgow Queen Street. The station was originally an island platform and had disappeared without trace.

On 22 January 1989, 43101, without its 'InterCity' logos, passes Fencehouses signal box on the diverted 0745 (Sun) Leeds–Glasgow Queen Street.

On 26 February 1989, 43043 passes the site of Fencehouses station on the diverted 1015 (Sun) Newcastle–Kings Cross.

On 12 March 1989, the second day of the eight-day Durham blockade, we see 47606 *Odin* approaching the site of Penshaw station on 1M76 the 1405 (Sun) Newcastle–Liverpool Lime Street. Note the gallery of photographers on the bridge!

The ECML was blocked between 11 and 19 March 1989 and all services diverted via Leamside. On Sunday 12 March we see 47231 *The Silcock Express* passing the site of Penshaw station (of which no trace remained at rail level) on the Wisbech–Deanside pet food train. The area to the left was once occupied by exchange sidings and the stationmaster's house can be seen in the right background above the rear of the train, marking the station site.

In its one-off LNER apple green livery, 47522 *Doncaster Enterprise* crosses the Victoria viaduct on the diverted 1142 (Sun) Newcastle–Liverpool Lime Street on 7 May 1989. The arch spanning the river has a span of 160 feet and is the only arch that is not a true semicircle. If you look carefully you can see it is a circular segment.

14 April 1991 was the last day of diversions via Leamside and on that afternoon, 43078 comes off the Victoria viaduct (which can be seen on the left) and approaches Washington on the diverted 1400 Kings Cross–Aberdeen. The former line to Consett ran across the foreground.

Another 14 April 1991 view as we see 43056 passing Washington on the diverted 1656 Newcastle–Kings Cross. The section over the Victoria viaduct had been singled many years previously. The station was beyond the footbridge in the background.

Class 158s only appeared on the line on a handful of occasions in early 1991 and on the last day of diversions, 14 April 1991, 158745 passes Washington on the diverted 1645 Newcastle–Liverpool Lime Street. This was the only photo I ever took of a 158 on the line.

On 22 January 1989, 31118 approaches the site of Washington station on an electrification train.

On the first day of the March 1989 blockade, Saturday 11 March, we see 47424 *The Brontës of Haworth* passing the site of Usworth station on the diverted 1403 Newcastle–Liverpool Lime Street. The station had almost completely disappeared without trace. The signal box can be seen in the background.

Although nominally freight-only, the Leamside line saw very little traffic of any kind in its last years except on days when ECML trains were diverted and so, paradoxically, it was more difficult to photograph freights on the line than passenger trains! On 11 March 1989, 37196 passes Wardley disposal point on 6N11 Tyne–Ferryhill trip.

5

Sunderland Area, South Hylton and on to Gateshead

The Sunderland area is another that has a long and complex railway history.

We will first travel to South Hylton, on the former line to Durham, now used by Tyne & Wear Metro trains but which is owned and maintained by Network Rail. The line from Hendon (on the South Dock branch) to Pallion remained open for freight until 1984 and was subsequently lifted.

Trains to South Hylton leave Sunderland station in a southerly direction and take a sharp curve to the west, following the route of the former line to Durham. This area was once occupied by Fawcett Street stabling sidings and two have been retained. The line then enters a short tunnel in which Park Lane station is located. This is located at the site of Fawcett Street Junction, where the line from Hendon, the docks and the former Fawcett Street station trailed in on the south side. Park Lane is also the city's main bus/Metro interchange.

Beyond Park Lane, the line follows the course of the former Durham line as it passes through University and Millfield stations. University is a new station whereas Millfield is built south-west of the site of the previous Millfield station, which closed on 1 May 1955, nine years before the rest of the line. A road overbridge carrying Hylton Road is immediately beyond the station and the previous station was beyond that bridge. At this point, trains are running in a north-westerly direction towards South Hylton. In fact, it is built on the site of the first Millfield station, which was relocated in around 1890.

Beyond Millfield, the line heads north-west through an area once famous for its shipbuilding industry. It then turns towards the west as it runs parallel to the River Wear and reaches Pallion station. This section of the line is north of the previous alignment, which had previously been lost to a new road (European Way). The old station was immediately south of and parallel to the new one on the other side of European Way. Also near here is the Queen Alexandra Bridge, built as a double-deck rail and road bridge in 1909 to allow coal trains from the Washington area to reach South Dock without reversal but which proved to be a white elephant – the railway closed in around 1921 but the bridge is still an important part of the city's road network. It is worth alighting at Pallion and walking to the bridge to appreciate its sheer size. The only trace of the old station is a bridge which once carried the railway over the nearby Merle Terrace and is now used as a footpath.

Beyond Pallion, the line heads in a south-westerly direction with glimpses of the River Wear to the north until it reaches the single-platform terminus at South Hylton. The line beyond to Penshaw is now a footpath and Penshaw itself is around 2 ½ miles away.

Returning to Sunderland, trains towards Newcastle leave the subterranean station through Sunderland North Tunnel and then, on leaving the tunnel, cross the River Wear on the Wearmouth Bridge – the road bridge is adjacent. St Peter's Metro station is immediately north of the bridge. This was used as a temporary terminus during early 2001 while North Tunnel was being prepared for electrification. A bus service ran between St Peter's and Sunderland stations. The station is of pre-fabricated construction.

Immediately north of St Peter's is the former Monkwearmouth station. This was built in 1848 in a grandiose Doric style, similar to but smaller than the more well-known station at Huddersfield, to impress the town's MP, 'Railway King' George Hudson. It closed in 1967 when the Sunderland–South Shields service ceased and reopened as a museum of local transport history in 1973, although it closed in 2017 owing to the building being in poor condition.

There were once extensive yards at Monkwearmouth and a short branch diverged inland to serve Wearmouth Colliery and many shipyards; the colliery was the last source of traffic on the branch until it closed in 1993. The site of the colliery, which was the last surviving pit in the county, is now Sunderland FC's 'Stadium of Light'. This is so named because the pitch is on the site of one of the pit shafts and 'to see the light' was a term used by miners when they came back to the surface at the end of their shift. Needless to say, supporters of Sunderland's arch-rivals Newcastle have a rather less than complimentary name for the stadium!

The next station is Stadium of Light, which was built as part of the Sunderland Metro project. It comprises breezeblock shelters on each platform.

The line heads in a northerly direction beyond Stadium of Light and enters a cutting, in which Seaburn station is located. This opened in 1937 to serve the residential developments that had started to be built in the area, as well as Sunderland FC's former stadium at Roker Park and the seaside districts of Seaburn and Roker. It is actually located in the village of Fulwell, which is known for its windmill. This can be glimpsed on the west side of the line from passing trains and is open to visitors. The station was completely rebuilt for the Metro and no trace of the original station remains.

Beyond Seaburn, the line heads in a north-westerly direction towards East Boldon station. By the late 1980s, all the buildings had been demolished and replaced with brick shelters. The NER signal box remained until resignalling for the Metro and was unusual in that the adjacent level crossing had manually controlled lifting barriers operated by a wheel in the signal box. The station was rebuilt for the Metro. As an aside, a BR NE Region tangerine sign pointing towards the station remained in place attached to a lamp post in the nearby village for many years, disappearing in around 2000.

Beyond East Boldon, the line continues in a straight direction heading north-west and passes Tile Shed AHB level crossing. Immediately beyond this was Tile Shed Junction, where a connecting line diverged northwards to Tyne Dock. This was used by Sunderland–South Shields trains until they were withdrawn on 2 March 1967.

The line curves slightly to take a more easterly course and passes over Boldon AHB level crossing and passes Boldon East Junction, where a new spur (opened in 1985) allows direct access from the Sunderland direction to Tyne Dock. This allowed coal trains from the Durham coalfield to use the new Tyne Coal Terminal, which could handle larger ships than Sunderland South Dock. Shortly afterwards, the line passes the site of Pontop Crossing, where the Stanhope & Tyne line from Washington to Tyne Dock crossed on the level. A disused lattice steel viaduct can be seen immediately south of the line, marking the course of the S&T line. As mentioned in chapter 4, the most famous traffic to use it was the Tyne Dock–Consett iron ore trains until 1966, when the line was closed between Washington North Junction and Boldon Colliery. The remaining stub remained open after the colliery had closed in 1982 to allow stocks to be removed. The crossing itself remained in situ for a few more years and was removed in around 1988 after all coal stocks at Boldon had been removed.

The line to Tyne Dock heads north for around half a mile before reaching the site of Green Lane Junction, where the now disused Stanhope & Tyne line to South Shields, latterly used by coal trains to Westoe Colliery, diverged to the north-east. The Tyne Dock line continues for around a mile, crossing the A194 road, before terminating in the docks complex. This was latterly the site for the Tyne Coal Terminal but the principal rail traffic to Tyne Dock is now imported biomass. For a brief period in the late 1990s there was also a daily intermodal train to/from Mossend, but this was not a success and was soon withdrawn.

Brockley Whins station, renamed from Boldon Colliery in July 1991, is around half a mile to the east of Boldon East Junction and the line from Tyne Dock trails in on the north side. The station was rebuilt for electrification and as part of this, the Down platform was relocated eastwards. It is now in the standard style used at Stadium of Light and East Boldon stations. A standard NER signal box remained in use until electrification.

East of Brockley Whins, the line continues on an embankment in an easterly direction; Fellgate station opened for Metro traffic on 31 March 2002 and is of the same style as the previous three.

Beyond Fellgate, the line continues in a straight easterly direction until the set of junctions at Pelaw is reached. A flying junction allows Metro trains to leave the Sunderland line and join the Metro line from South Shields, which crosses the Sunderland and Leamside lines on separate skew bridges before descending to run past Pelaw reversing sidings and parallel to the Sunderland line. The Network Rail freight-only line from Jarrow trails in on the north side.

Pelaw station is immediately beyond the sidings and consists of an island platform served only by Metro trains. The original plans for the Metro did not include a station here but it was not long before it opened on 16 September 1985. The original station was of the style adopted for almost all the new or rebuilt stations on the Metro, comprising curved platform canopies, but was replaced by a larger and very distinctive new building in 2006.

The southern (slow) pair of lines from Pelaw to Newcastle was once electrified on the 600 V DC third rail system as part of the LNER's electrification scheme to South Shields. This had been commissioned in 1938 but was abandoned in 1963 owing to a significant decline in traffic. The similarly electrified North Tyne circle, which had been electrified in 1904, was also de-electrified a few years later in 1967 but both the South Shields line and North Tyne circle are now electrified again as part of the Metro.

East of Pelaw, the line runs in a deep cutting for around half a mile. Heworth station is located in this cutting and opened on 5 November 1979 before the Metro opened to here from the Newcastle direction on 15 November 1981. It is a bus/rail/Metro interchange but wins no prizes for its architecture (unless you like lots of bare concrete!). The Metro platforms are covered but the Network Rail platforms are open and windswept.

The line continues in a north-westerly direction past Felling station. This comprises an island platform serving the Metro only. The original Brandling Junction Railway station building is visible on the north side of the line. Gateshead Stadium, which is also only served by the Metro, is around half a mile beyond and the athletics stadium can be seen on the north side of the line.

At Gateshead Stadium, the Metro line turns to the south and enters the tunnel that takes it through Gateshead and beyond. The main line continues westwards, passing the disused Tyneside Central Freight Terminal, which closed in the early 1990s, on the north side, and then takes a 90-degree turn to face south-west, before turning again through the site of Gateshead East station (the former Gateshead West station can be seen to the south) to face north and crossing the Tyne via the High Level Bridge to reach Newcastle.

On 20 May 1989, 47424 *The Brontës of Haworth* leaves Sunderland on the 1530 Newcastle–Middlesbrough Pacer replacer. This was the last year that such services ran in the North East.

Sunderland station was not a particularly inspiring place following the 1960s rebuilding but at least you could see daylight from the platforms, unlike its successor! On 20 May 1989, 101339 awaits departure from Sunderland on the 1215 to Newcastle.

On 24 February 2001, Sunderland station is being rebuilt as 153359 leaves on the 1030 York–Newcastle via Middlesbrough. The single-island platform was widened over the formation of the original Down line and the new Down line can be seen on the left.

Sunderland is in transition on 5 May 2001 as 156484 leaves on the 1300 Newcastle–York. Fawcett Street sidings have been temporarily removed to facilitate the building of the new Metro line to South Hylton.

On 4 July 2004, we see the gloomy new Sunderland station as 4001 (with 4026 just visible behind) stop on the 'Tyneside Centenarian' tour, awaiting departure towards Newcastle. The tour marked the centenary of the first NER electric trains on the North Tyne circle. The station has seen significant improvements at platform level since then.

On 4 August 2003, 4020, sporting an advertising livery promoting modern apprenticeships, stops at Pallion on a train from South Hylton. At this time, a number of Metrocars sported advertising liveries.

On the early morning of 31 March 2002, the first day of the Sunderland Metro service, 4001 has just arrived at South Hylton on the first passenger-carrying train. In spite of the early hour, the train carried quite a few passengers, many of whom were, unsurprisingly, enthusiasts! This set carried a 'retro' Tyne & Wear livery for many years.

On 14 May 1988, a 101 has left Sunderland North Tunnel and crossed the Wearmouth Bridge as it approaches Monkwearmouth on the 1115 Sunderland–Newcastle. The 'Well Done The Lads' banner refers to Sunderland FC, which had just been promoted from the Third to the Second Division. The train is passing the site of the new St Peter's station.

On 3 August 1991, 142520 crosses the Wearmouth Bridge on the 0930 Newcastle–Middlesbrough. The tower of Wearmouth Colliery is in the left background and St Peter's station has since been built north of the bridge.

This NER lower quadrant semaphore signal was a feature of Monkwearmouth museum for many years and makes an interesting contrast with a class 108 passing on the 1005 Metro Centre–Sunderland on 3 August 1991.

During the summer of 1994, the Wearmouth Bridge was renovated and this required single line working between Monkwearmouth and Sunderland, using first the Up line and then the Down. On 23 July 1994, 142020 and a 156 head south through Monkwearmouth on the 1254 Newcastle–Middlesbrough.

In the spring of 2001, trains from Newcastle terminated at St Peter's to allow installation of overhead line equipment in Sunderland North Tunnel. On 10 March, 156451 has just arrived at St Peter's and will form the 1315 to Metro Centre. A bus shuttle service, operated by Stagecoach, was provided between the two stations but as they are only ½ mile apart, many passengers were quite happy to walk!

The proximity of St Peter's and Monkwearmouth stations is apparent as 4005 passes Monkwearmouth on a southbound train – the photo was taken from St Peter's station. Sadly, the electrification works meant that visitors to the museum could no longer use the footbridge, causing the loss of a good photographic location. The footbridge does make for an interesting contrast with the Metrocar!

On 27 July 2002, 4001 leaves St Peter's for South Hylton. Sunderland FC's Stadium of Light can be seen in the background.

On 4 July 2003, 20302 and 20301 pass St Peter's on 6E44 Sellafield–Hartlepool power station flasks.

On 22 March 2003, 4036 leaves Stadium of Light station for Newcastle.

On 6 July 1991, 143622 arrives at Seaburn on the 1345 Newcastle–Sunderland. The wooden platforms remained until the station was rebuilt for the Metro.

On 28 July 2001, work is well underway at Seaburn for the introduction of Metro services as 156454 arrives on the 1045 Sunderland–Metro Centre.

On 15 February 2003, 4061, sporting a promotional livery for the Connexions careers service, stops at Seaburn on a train to South Hylton.

On 17 October 1993, 47578 passes East Boldon on the ecs of a Sunderland–Middlesbrough footex.

On 12 March 1995, 156512 stops at East Boldon on the 1100 (Sundays) Newcastle–Middlesbrough. Strathclyde-liveried 156s would occasionally be seen on North East local services. This was most likely to happen on Sundays as a Scottish 156 would arrive at Newcastle on a Saturday evening on a train from Glasgow via Carlisle but had no booked work until the Monday morning, so would sometimes be purloined by Heaton depot to work local trains on a Sunday!

On 22 March 2003, a Metro train is seen near Pontop Crossing heading for South Hylton. Car 4042, advertising Metro Radio, leads.

On 31 March 1990, 143601 passes Boldon Colliery signal box on the 1030 Newcastle–Middlesbrough.

On 5 May 1990, 31120 passes Boldon Colliery on a Middlesbrough–Newcastle footex.

On 9 February 1997, 37708 is seen at Brockley Whins, as it had now been renamed, on a pway. There were three pway trains parked nose to tail, with 37248 (typically unphotographable!) and 56039 behind this train, all waiting for a possession in the Gateshead area to be lifted to allow them to return to Tyne Yard.

A short-lived working during 1999/2000 was 4S45 Tyne Dock–Mossend intermodal. On 12 March 2000, we see the very unusual combination of 66118 and 47738 *Bristol Barton Hill* coming off the Tyne Dock branch at Brockley Whins on this train.

On 1 September 2001, 156454 stops at Brockley Whins on the 1203 Metro Centre–Sunderland. The new Down platform is complete on the right and awaits commissioning.

On 10 March 2002, 4062 passes the now disused signal box at Brockley Whins on a crew-training run. This was demolished shortly afterwards.

On 9 March 1989, 47454 passes Pelaw on the 1142 (Sundays) Newcastle–Liverpool Lime Street, which was diverted via the Leamside line.

On 27 January 1990, 56118 is seen at Pelaw heading for Wardley on mgr empties. The BR 'large logo' livery suited these locomotives well.

On 14 November 1992, 47212 passes Pelaw on 6E18 Stanlow–Jarrow petrol.

On 27 March 1993, Metrocar 4087, which was the prototype for the refurbishment programme and painted in a one-off livery, is seen at Pelaw on a terminating service from the coastal circle.

On a snowy 19 February 1994, 156464 passes Pelaw on the 0835 Carlisle–Middlesbrough. 4018 has arrived at the Metro station on a terminating service.

On 23 May 1997, 47798 *Prince William* takes the empty Royal Train into Pelaw up loop after conveying HM The Queen and HRH The Duke of Edinburgh to Newcastle on an official visit to the North East.

On 5 August 2000, West Yorkshire 158906 passes Pelaw on the 0822 Liverpool Lime Street–Sunderland. 4070 has just arrived on a terminating Metro service.

On 12 December 2001,
47764 *Resounding* and
47793 *St Augustine* top
and tail a test train at
Pelaw.

On a snowy 31 December
2001, 4023 (in green
livery) and 4081 (in
blue) pass the ongoing
works to build the new
junction at Pelaw for
Sunderland trains.

On 29 March 1992, 47634
Holbeck passes Heworth
on a Newcastle–
Sunderland footex.

On 21 October 2000, Metro ran some trains formed of three cars to accommodate crowds wishing to see the Great North Run. I believe this was the first time that three-car trains operated and the motors of the centre car had to be cut out as the power supply cannot support three-car operation. One such train, with 4076 leading, approaches Heworth bound for South Shields.

On 21 March 1992, 47492 passes Felling on the ecs of a Sunderland–Bristol Temple Meads footex.

On 25 November 1995, Metrocar 4045 arrives at Felling on a train for Pelaw. It is sporting the second experimental 'refurbished' livery, which was also carried by 4039 and 4087.

On 25 October 1998, Metro battery loco BL1 is seen at Felling during a possession as 156463 passes on the 1300 Newcastle–Sunderland. Attitudes were more laid-back in those days; nowadays there would be fences and security guards preventing access to the station.

On 10 September 1988, 37350 approaches Gateshead Stadium on the return leg of 1Z36, Pathfinder Tours' 'The Tynesider' tour from Reading via Bristol to the Blyth & Tyne. The class 08 on the right is the depot pilot for the Tyneside Central Freight Terminal, which closed a few years later.

Also on 10 September 1988, 31409 approaches Gateshead Stadium on the 1458 Middlesbrough–Newcastle Pacer replacer.

On a dull Sunday 31 May 1998, 56010 passes Gateshead Stadium on a ballast train to Tyne Yard – there had been a possession between Newcastle and Heworth that day. Note the staff riding on the wagons, a practice that is no longer permitted!

6

Jarrow and South Shields

As previously mentioned, this line was electrified between 1938 and 1963 on the 600 V DC third rail system. It closed to BR traffic on 1 June 1981 and reopened to Metro trains on 24 March 1984.

Returning to Pelaw, a Metro train to South Shields departs the station and passes the reversing sidings immediately beyond, briefly heading east before the line climbs over the Leamside and Durham Coast lines, at which point the connections allowing Metro trains to join the coast line diverge to the east. The NR freight-only line to Jarrow now runs parallel to the line, which becomes single track for around a mile. The River Tyne can be glimpsed to the north as the line heads in a north-easterly direction before the long passing loop on which Hebburn station is reached. This area was once famous for shipbuilding and some ship repair yards remained in business during the 1990s.

Beyond Hebburn, the line becomes single track again as it heads eastwards towards Jarrow, where there is also a passing loop. The NR freight line bypasses the station to the north. Jarrow is famous for the 1936 Jarrow March, when a delegation of unemployed former shipyard workers walked to London to ask the government for help at a time of very severe economic hardship. There is a monument to the march on the Newcastle-bound platform at the station.

Immediately beyond Jarrow station, the line becomes single track again for around half a mile until the line to the oil terminal diverges to the north; the Metro line becomes double track again at this point. Both lines then cross the approach roads to the Tyne Tunnels on separate bridges and the oil terminal can be seen briefly, before the line takes a south-easterly direction to reach the next station, Bede.

The section from Jarrow to Bede and Tyne Dock Tunnel was originally single track but after freight services to Simonside wagon works were withdrawn in the late 1980s, the second track became disused and in March 1993 the Metro took the second track over and electrified it, allowing an increase in service frequency on the South Shields line from every ten to every seven–eight minutes.

The next station, Simonside, is only a short distance away and opened on 17 March 2008. No trace of the former wagon works can be seen from the line, which now turns to take a north-easterly direction through Tyne Dock tunnel (the line from Brockley Whins to Tyne Dock passes over this tunnel) as two disused lines, the former Stanhope & Tyne line from Green Lane Junction and the line from Tile Shed Junction, met as they trailed in on the east side as the line heads in a northerly direction.

The disused line now runs parallel to the Metro line as Tyne Dock station is approached. The two lines diverged south of Tyne Dock station, which was rebuilt on the former Stanhope & Tyne formation for the Metro; the BR station was just to the west. Beyond Tyne Dock, the original British Railways (originally Brandling Junction Railway) line ran along a more easterly route through High Shields but little trace now remains.

Dean Road exchange sidings were located on the BR line a short distance north of Tyne Dock and marked the boundary between BR and the National Coal Board. The NCB lines were electrified at 500 V dc overhead beyond here and trains from Westoe would be worked by NCB locomotives and handed over to BR locos at this point. In 1988, the line was upgraded to allow class 56 locomotives and MGR wagons to run all the way to Westoe colliery (coal traffic from Westoe had largely been taken away by ship via Harton Low staithes on the River Tyne prior to then) and the electrification along this section was abandoned. A short section of the Westoe system, including the electrification, remained in use between the colliery and Harton Low Staithes, for colliery waste to be transferred to ships, but this was abandoned in 1989 and replaced by a conveyor; the colliery itself closed in 1993. This was a particularly fascinating line to visit and in its last years, a friendly approach at the entrance gate would always result in an invitation to have a look around and even a ride if you were lucky!

The next station, Chichester (pronounced with a long 'I', unlike the Sussex city), is also a bus/rail interchange. The NCB line to Westoe diverged to the east just after Chichester station and the Metro line then continues on a concrete viaduct over the former NCB yards before terminating at South Shields.

The present Metro station at South Shields is the town's second Metro station. The new station is south of the former one and although further from the town centre, offers a better interchange between the Metro and buses. The line remains in situ through the site of the previous Metro station and on to the site of the BR station, now used as sidings and a footpath runs alongside the line from the entrances to the old station as far as the new.

The BR station at South Shields was once an attractive structure with an overall roof but was allowed to become derelict during the 1960s although, unlike all the other intermediate stations on the line, remained staffed until closure on 1 June 1981. The roof was soon removed but the buildings remained until the late 1990s when they were demolished. The BR station was in fact the fourth station to serve the town, having opened in 1879 and replacing previous stations which had existed between 1842–79, 1839–42 and 1835–39. As a result, the first Metro station became the town's fifth and the second is therefore the town's sixth! Few other towns of similar size can have been served by so many stations over time.

Railtours have visited the Jarrow line on a number of occasions. On 10 September 1994, we see 47616 (with 56090 at the rear) on the short section of double track west of Hebburn on 1F52, Hertfordshire Railtours' 'Blyth Spirit III' from Kings Cross, which also visited the Blyth & Tyne.

On 9 December 1995, 60047 *Robert Owen* passes Hebburn on 6M19 Jarrow–Stanlow petrol empties. The Metro line is in the foreground.

On 10 September 1994, we see 56090 (with 47616 at the rear) passing Jarrow on 1F52, Hertfordshire Railtours' 'Blyth Spirit III' tour.

On a cold 27 November 1993, 37711 approaches Jarrow station on 6M19 Jarrow–Stanlow petrol empties. Over the years, these trains used 47s, then 37s and finally 60s, before the traffic was largely lost to coastal shipping.

The branch into the Jarrow oil terminal crosses over the roundabout at the south end of the Tyne Tunnel. On 13 May 2000, we see the very unusual sight of 56032 shunting at the terminal having arrived on the morning working from Immingham, which had replaced Stanlow as the source of traffic a few years previously. This was the only time I ever saw a class 56 on this duty, which by this time was almost always a class 60. To take this shot involved dashing across the lanes of traffic at the roundabout as there was no other means of getting into the middle. I suspect health and safety would frown on this sort of activity these days!

On the night of 13 March 1993, we see Metro battery loco BL2 (BL1 and BL3 were at the other end) at Bede on an engineers' train in conjunction with the commissioning of the double track between Jarrow and Bede, back in the days when night photography required a tripod and long time exposure. In my experience, Metro staff were generally quite obliging about letting you onto stations to photograph works trains such as this in a possession as long as you kept away from the actual worksite.

On the morning of Sunday 30 October 1994, an emergency exercise took place on the Metro between Tyne Dock and Chichester stations on 30 October 1994. The scenario was that a passenger train (153357) had collided head-on with a freight (one mgr wagon and 56108, which were out of sight to the left) and a Metro train (4068) had ploughed into the wreckage. Here we see the 'scene' as the exercise nears its end. The 153 was almost at the end of the former Westoe branch; a sleeper was tied to the rails at the former BR/NCB boundary just out of view and the track had been lifted on the NCB's side of the boundary! I believe this is the only time a second generation DMU ever travelled on this line.

On 17 May 1998, 4087, sporting a 'Seaside Special' livery, arrives at South Shields. The previous station is to the left and the new one to the right. As a result, trains no longer cross this bridge in passenger service.

On 29 June 1998, 4018 awaits departure from the original Metro station at South Shields. The view is looking towards the sidings and former BR station. By this time, very few Metrocars carried the old yellow and white livery.

On 10 March 1990, we see 4044 and 4051 in South Shields sidings during a photo-stop on SWS Enterprises' 'The Tynesider' tour, which covered the majority of the Metro network. The cars had been painted in liveries representing the Brandling Junction Railway (yellow) and Newcastle and North Shields Railway (crimson) to mark 150 years since these two lines first opened. They usually ran coupled together. These sidings are on the site of the former BR station.

On 13 March 1993, we see Metro battery locos BL1 and BL3 (BL2 was at the other end) in South Shields sidings, awaiting being called to the worksite at Bede that evening, in connection with the commissioning of the double track section between there and Jarrow.

Not long before the electric railway at Westoe/Harton closed (to be replaced by a conveyor), we see electric loco 13 shunting at Harton staithes on 13 July 1989. This was a fascinating railway and the staff very friendly. I was even invited up for a ride!

7

Bishop Auckland and Weardale

The line to Bishop Auckland and Weardale is the sole survivor of a once extensive network of lines in the west of County Durham. It is steeped in history, with a part of it comprising the former Stockton & Darlington Railway.

Trains depart Darlington heading north and at Parkgate Junction, around half a mile north, diverge to the west. This section of line is single track. It joins the course of the S&D just west of Parkgate Junction and the line then follows a north-westerly direction. Running on an embankment, the line crosses the River Skerne on a single-arch bridge built by Ignatius Bonomi of Durham, one of the first railway architects and famously shown on the former George Stephenson £5 note. The bridge is listed as a Scheduled Monument.

Shortly afterwards, trains arrive at North Road station, where only one platform remains in use. The majority of the station is now the Head of Steam museum; it was converted to a museum in 1975 as part of the 150th anniversary celebrations of the Stockton & Darlington Railway and is well worth a visit. As the train heads north from North Road, the former line to Barnard Castle and Stainmore diverged to the west and Darlington Works was on the east side. The site of the works is now occupied by a Morrison's supermarket and a brick art form representing the famous A4 Pacific *Mallard* is included in the site.

The line then heads north out of Darlington into open countryside, crossing the A1(M). Around a mile to the north, the test track for the new Hitachi train factory appears on the west side and the connections to the new factory can be seen just before the train arrives at Heighington station, where the line becomes double track again.

Heighington (the 'e' is silent) still retains its signal box and semaphores and is famous as being the place where the locomotive *Locomotion* was first put on rails and steamed, having been taken from Newcastle by road. The original station, which was a pub for many years, is on the east (up) side and part of the station's original low platform can be seen in front of it.

The station is around a mile from the village that it serves and is nearer to Aycliffe than Heighington – new platforms were built during the Second World War, staggered either side of the level crossing, for the benefit of workers at a nearby munitions factory. The platforms had generous but austere canopies but these were removed in the mid-1990s. The area remains industrial to this day and has been incorporated into the New Town of Newton Aycliffe.

The line continues northwards, skirting Newton Aycliffe, and then turns to take a direction slightly north of west, as it passes the site of Simpasture Junction, where the Clarence Railway line from Stillington Junction trailed in on the north side. Simpasture Junction is believed to be the first junction between two competing companies. It will be recalled that the line from Stillington had been electrified by the NER at 1500 V dc in 1915 (abandoned 1935). The austere Newton Aycliffe station is located here.

The line is now straight for around 2 miles as it approaches Shildon. The approaches to the station were once dominated by the NER's marshalling yards but these finally closed, after a long decline, when Shildon wagon works closed in 1984. Much of the site of the Down side yards is now occupied by the NRM's new 'Locomotion' museum, which is well worth a visit. The town itself is also well worth a visit to any student of railway history.

Shildon station is on a curve as the line changes course and heads in a north-westerly direction. The station still retains semaphore signalling and an attractive NER signal box. Beyond the station, the line becomes single track through Shildon Tunnel and emerging from the tunnel, passes the outskirts of Bishop Auckland, before turning to take a westerly route and terminating at the station.

Bishop Auckland station now boasts only a single platform but at one time covered an extensive area. It was a junction station for trains from Ferryhill, Durham and Darlington and on to Weardale and north-west Durham. Although there was a triangular junction layout, the station did not have platforms on the western side of the triangle. All this has now gone and a supermarket occupies the redundant land.

The line beyond into Weardale is now owned by the Weardale Railway. Its story has been documented elsewhere and it is not intended to describe it in this book although mention will be made of the works carried out at the stations.

The line beyond Bishop Auckland was used by trains to Crook, Tow Law and Blackhill, where it joined the network of lines serving Consett, as well as Eastgate and Wearhead. Services to Blackhill ceased on 1 May 1939, to Tow Law on 11 June 1956 and Crook on 8 March 1965. The line to Wearhead closed to passengers on 29 June 1953 and closed completely beyond the Eastgate cement works in stages between 1961 and 1965. The line remained busy with cement traffic to Eastgate until the works closed in 1993 and for five consecutive summers between 1988 and 1992 (inclusive), a Sunday service ran as far as Stanhope for the benefit of daytrippers.

Beyond Bishop Auckland, the line heads in a north-westerly direction past the Weardale Railway's Bishop Auckland West platform. The first station was Etherley, which closed with the cessation of services to Crook. It remained intact after closure and reopened for the summer Sunday service as 'Witton Park' in 1991. The line continues in a north-easterly direction and crosses the River Wear on a spectacular viaduct, before reaching the site of Wear Valley Junction station, closed on 8 July 1935. At this point, the line to Crook and beyond headed north while the Weardale line took a sharp curve to head in an easterly direction towards Witton-le-Wear as it tried to find the best means to follow the valley of the River Wear, which from here to the end of the line, is never far from the line and can often be seen.

Witton-le-Wear station was located by a skew level crossing with protecting semaphore signals. The original station was demolished but a replacement platform was provided by the Weardale Railway. Beyond Witton-le-Wear, the line turns towards the north-west for the next 3 or so miles, passing the site of Harperley station, before turning to head due west and arriving at Wolsingham, where the station remained as a private house. A new station was subsequently built by the Weardale Railway.

Beyond Wolsingham, the line heads almost due west for around 3 miles as it follows the River Wear, crossing it on a steel girder bridge around half a mile east of Frosterley station, where the original station also remained as a private house. As at Wolsingham, the Weardale Railway built a new platform here.

Beyond Frosterley, the line heads in a north-westerly direction for around 1 ½ miles until it reaches the attractive small town of Stanhope (pronounced 'Stan'up'), which was the terminus of the short-lived summer Sunday service. The station remained intact but very shabby; the Weardale Railway subsequently restored it and reinstated the platform canopies.

Beyond Stanhope, the line continues in a westerly direction, crossing the Wear for the last time around a mile west of the station, before passing the site of Eastgate station and terminating at the former cement works just beyond. The line continued for another 6 ½ miles to Wearhead, where it terminated, with intermediate stations at Westgate and St John's Chapel.

The names 'Eastgate' and 'Westgate' refer to the fact that these communities marked the eastern and western boundaries of the private hunting forest of the Prince Bishops of Durham.

On 18 April 1993, 142018 stops at Heighington on the 0921 Saltburn–Bishop Auckland. The new Hitachi factory was subsequently built in the right of the background.

The last train to Eastgate before closure was Pathfinders' 'Weardale Explorer' tour from Bath Spa on 10 April 1993. It is seen approaching Shildon on the outward leg with 37506 *British Steel Skinningrove* and 37512 *Thornaby Demon* hauling it. 47513 *Severn* was at the rear. The wasteland on the right was once part of Shildon yard and is now occupied by the NRM 'Locomotion' centre.

On 31 December 1994, LMS class 2 2-6-0 46441 worked two return trips from Darlington to Stanhope to publicise the proposed reopening of the Eastgate line (which subsequently led to the Weardale Railway). The second of these is seen approaching Shildon.

On 2 April 1996, the ecs of the Royal Train passes Shildon en route to Wolverton. It had conveyed HRH The Prince of Wales to Bishop Auckland. 47798 *Prince William* is at the head of the train. 47799 *Prince Henry* was at the rear.

On a snowy 7 March 1987, 143004 awaits departure from Bishop Auckland on the 1027 to Saltburn. The new station had just been completed. The line to Eastgate can be seen on the right.

On 20 March 1993, 37509 is seen crossing Etherley viaduct on the return leg of 1Z38, Black Cat Railtours' 'Farewell to Eastgate' tour from Crewe. 37707 and 37708 were at the rear.

On 20 March 1993, 37708 and 37707 are seen at Witton-le-Wear level crossing on 1Z38, Black Cat Railtours' 'Farewell to Eastgate' tour from Crewe. 37509 was at the rear. The low line speeds meant that it was possible to chase this tour in my car!

To publicise a proposed reopening of the Eastgate line (which ultimately led to the Weardale Railway), 2005 and 47833/D1962 worked two specials from Darlington to Eastgate on 8 March 1993. Here we see the first train just west of Witton-le-Wear on the outward run to Eastgate.

On 27 February 1993, there are traces of snow on the ground (but no sun!) as 43073 approaches Witton-le-Wear on the return leg of 1G06, Hertfordshire Railtours' 'Tyne & Wear 125 Special' from Kings Cross, which visited both Eastgate and Newcastle. This was the last HST to visit the branch. The River Wear can be seen in the left background.

On 17 February 1990, 43013 crosses the River Wear east of Frosterley heading for Bishop Auckland on 1Z14, Hertfordshire Railtours' 'Wear and Tees 125 Special', which also visited Saltburn. This power car is now part of the New Measurement Train.

Frosterley station is now an attractive private house. On 11 November 1989 43060 passes on 1Z28, Hertfordshire Railtours' 'Wear and Tees 125 Special' from St Pancras, which also visited Saltburn.

On 22 May 1988, a 101 is seen at Stanhope on the 0900 from Darlington. This was the first day of the new summer service to Weardale, which ran until the end of the 1992 summer timetable. The service was popular and connecting buses allowed passengers to travel to other tourist destinations such as the Killhope Wheel lead mining museum and Alston.

The 1980s seem like another world, where passengers were allowed off railtours at closed stations and no one minded people walking along the tracks. On 11 November 1989 43060 stops at Stanhope on 1Z28, Hertfordshire Railtours' 'Wear and Tees 125 Special' from St Pancras. The NER footbridge acted as an unofficial right of way across the railway and makes an interesting contrast with the train.

On 3 April 1993, 37512 *Thornaby Demon* (with 47817 at the rear) is seen at Eastgate on NENTA's 'Weardale Valley Ghost' tour from Norwich. The line continued beyond the station to the cement works but the tour terminated at the station.

On 18 May 1993, 31547 and inspection saloon are seen at Eastgate on a VIP special from Doncaster in connection with the proposed re-opening of the line as the Weardale Railway. Participants enjoyed a lunch break here.

8

Raisby Hill

By the late 1980s, the Raisby Hill branch was all that remained of the former line from Ferryhill to Hart, which as mentioned in chapters 1 and 4, closed on 9 June 1952. The line had remained open for general freight and to serve to Raisby Hill Quarry but all traffic had ceased by the late 1980s and the line has since been closed and lifted.

The line diverged from the ECML around half a mile north of Ferryhill and turned to the east, passing the site of West Cornforth station, where there was a trainman-operated level crossing, around a quarter of a mile after leaving the ECML. The station remained open for freight traffic until 30 September 1963. The disused platforms remained in situ until the final closure of the line. The line then headed eastwards, passing under the A1(M) motorway until it reached the site of Coxhoe Bridge station (around 1 ½ miles from West Cornforth), at the point where the line was crossed by the A177 road bridge. No trace remained of the station at track level. The line then continued on to the quarry around a mile to the east.

I only ever photographed two railtours on the line, which is now largely forgotten. The tracks were lifted in the mid-90s.

I believe that 1Z39, Pathfinders' 'North Eastender' tour from the Bristol area of 16 March 1991 was the last to visit the line; it also visited Eastgate and the Leamside line. The train used 37214 and 47828 at each end and is seen at West Cornforth on the outward leg. The station was to the left of 37214.

On 9 September 1990, 47474 *Sir Rowland Hill*, with 47533 at the rear, approaches the site of Coxhoe Bridge station on 1Z30, the Branch Line Society's 'Tyne Tees Wanderer' from Manchester Piccadilly to Sunderland South Dock (see photo in chapter 3), Raisby Hill, Lackenby and Redcar Mineral Terminal. It is seen on the outward run, heading for the quarry.

Acknowledgments

Grateful thanks are offered to all those railway staff at BR, its successors and the Tyne & Wear Metro, who kept me informed of newsworthy events in that long-ago era before mobile telephones, gen groups and Real Time Trains! I would also like to thank my then employers for their forbearance when I would ask for leave at often very short notice because something interesting was scheduled to happen!

Grateful thanks are also offered to the webmaster of the Six Bells Junction site (www. sixbellsjunction.co.uk) for all the information about the various railtours featured in this book.